Ukraine and the Art of Strategy